TABLE OF CONTENTS

I0420284

LIST OF ILLUSTRATIONS

INTRODUCTION

The Brazilian Amazon Region is, undeniably, an area of great geopolitical importance. This is easily perceived due to its inherent problems, resulting from a series of colliding realities, such as:

- Vast land area (5,000,000 square Km);

- Low population density (2.7 Inh/square Km);

- Long borders (11,248 Km);

- Richness in natural resources.

In recent years, that Region, among other environment issues, has been intensely discussed. Often, passion of the interests groups overlapped science, and half-truths were accepted as scientific knowledge.

As a result, Brazil has frequently been singled out in the past, by international opinion, as one of the most "ecologically incorrect" countries of the world, particularly in relation to development projects in the Amazon[1].

After these considerations, we intend to figure out why, suddenly, "the Amazon jungle" became so important for the world and how Brazil is dealing with the accusation of being the enemy of nature.

To achieve this objective, we will first give a brief introduction to the area and its settlement. After this important understanding, we will address some international attempts to control the exploitation of the region, including the creation of various stories and myths.

Finally, we will present the policies for that region and the actions that have been done by the Brazilian Government to ensure that its sovereignty over the Amazon is out of question.

AREA'S CHARACTERISTICS

Area's description

Known as "Green Continent", the entire amazon region covers an area of approximately 7,800,000 square Km. The region extends through the Equator and comprises the entire Amazon river basin and its tributaries.

This immense environment is of interest to seven other countries aside from Brazil: Surinam, Guyana, Venezuela, Colombia, Peru, Bolivia, and Ecuador.

This awesome size of the region is conveyed by the following figures[2]:

- 5 % of the world's land;

- 40 % of the South America;

- 20 % of the world's fresh water;

- 30 % of the world's jungle;

- 11,248 Km of international borders;

- 23,000 Km of navigable rivers;

- Distances of 2,000 Km (N-S) and 3,000 Km (E-W).

In 1978 a cooperation treaty was signed by these eight countries with interests in the Amazon region, with the purpose of establishing a joint program to develop the entire region. The treaty led to several conferences held in various countries.

"Legal Amazon Region" is the customary way in which the Brazilian Amazon Region is known. It includes, geographically, seven entire Brazilian states and part of the other two states, which together encompass an area equivalent to about 5,000,000 square Km^3, or 60% of the Brazilian territory (Fig 1 and 2).

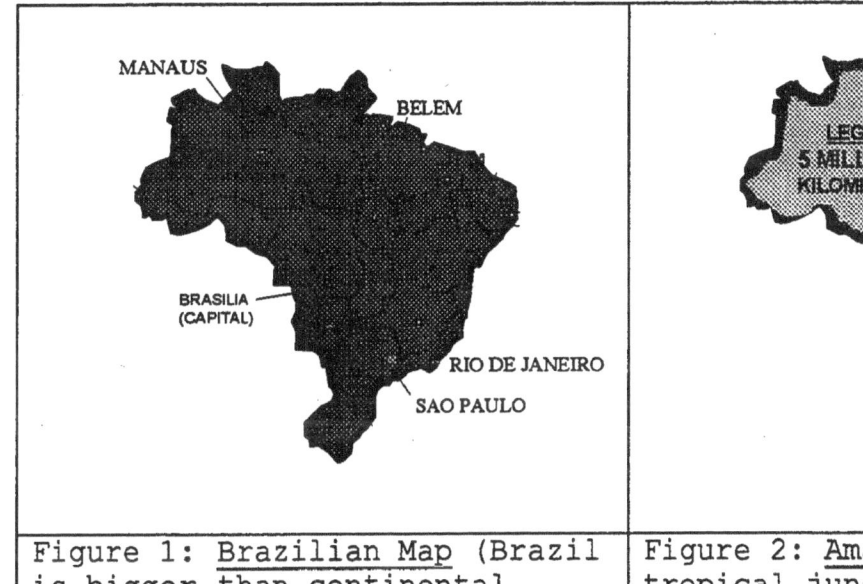 

Figure 1: <u>Brazilian Map</u> (Brazil is bigger than continental United States)	Figure 2: <u>Amazon Region</u> (The tropical jungle is 3,9 million square kilometer which represents 78% of Legal Amazon)

Population

This vast area is sparsely populated, with larger concentrations in important centers such as Manaus and Belem, cities with populations in excess of one million[4]. The area also includes more than 90% of the Indian reservation actually existent in Brazil. Most of them, however, are already experimenting integration with "civilization"[5].

3

Relief

The terrain is essentially composed of a large sedimentary basin, bordered to the north and south, respectively, by the Guianese and Brazilian Crystalline Shield, and east west from the Atlantic Ocean to the Andes range.

In the Guianese shield lies the highest peak found in Brazil - The Pico da Neblina (Foggy Summit) -, with an elevation of 3,014 meters.

Hydrography

The hydrography, the unrivaled worldwide phenomenon, includes the Amazon and Solimões basins along with the thousands of tributaries associated with them. They are, usually, the area's sole means of transportation. Traveling from one place to another, by river, may take several days, as for example from Manaus to Belem, that is about 1,300 Km distance, takes approximately four days.

Two thirds of the Brazilian hydroelectric reserves are located in the Amazon region[6].

Climate

The climate is characteristically tropical, with constant temperature throughout the year, and with very high annual indexes for average temperature (26°C or 80°F) and for precipitation (2,000 mm). There is, however, a drought season that lasts from five to six months. The temperatures, in themselves, are not very high; humidity, usually higher than 75%,

4

is largely responsible for the difficult lifestyle encountered in the Amazon region, prejudicing the settlement and the development in the area[7].

Vegetation

The vegetation cover is widely diversified and may be outlined as follows:

"varzea" forest or "Igapo", which is regularly flooded land or permanently submerged land; tropical jungle; transitional forest (semi-humid); other kinds of vegetation, like savanna, grassland, coastal vegetation, etc.[8].

It is worth emphasizing that the Amazon jungle lies within part (78%) of the Legal Amazon region, as showed in figure 2. According to the Brazilian National Space Research Institute (INPE), which monitors general deforestation through LANDSAT and SPOT remote sensing satellites images, about 90% of the Amazon jungle remains almost untouched[9].

This 280 million hectares of vegetation hold the biggest ecosystem found in Earth, possessing incomparable and opulent biodiversity.

"In an area of 2 square Kilometers, it can be found 300 different species of flora"[10].

However, although all the difficulties to live in the region, its mineral deposits, some with strategic worth, bring to the area the adventurers and international attention[11].

SETTLEMENT OF THE REGION

Since the beginning of Brazil's colonization, the conquest of the Amazon has been an episode written with courage and determination. Blood was spilled in combat in the jungle where the guerrilla warfare has been always present[12].

Thus, it was not a peaceful conquest. Violent disputes were fought by the Portuguese-Brazilian forces, in the XVII century, in order to expel English, French, Dutch and Irish, which had come for exploration and commerce and tried to dominate the land[13].

Although only nowadays may it be said that the region is in fact being settled, the beginning of its colonization period was in 1616, when the Portuguese Francisco Caldeira Castello Branco founded the city of Belem, in the state of Para, by building a fort.

In 1637, Captain Pedro Teixeira led a reconnaissance expedition to explore the Amazon River and reached the city of Quito, in Ecuador. The results obtained by his expedition served, much later, as the first argument in the doctrine of "Uti Possidetis" upon which the Treaty of Madrid of 1750 would confirm the Portuguese-Brazilian conquest[14].

During the XVII, XVIII and XIX centuries, thirty-seven fortifications had been established to defend the Amazon Region.

At the end of the XVII century, iron and brass cannons had already been mounted in Fort "São José do Rio Negro", which originated the city of Manaus, the main city of the Amazon Region.

It is important to emphasize that the military contingent of those fortifications constituted, for a many years, the only Portuguese-Brazilian civilization in the area. Subsequently, many of these Forts became today's cities and towns. In the XIX century the military colonies came into existence. Formed by military contingents assigned to protect the area and by a small civilian group, they became the main population in those locations. The first military colony was founded in 1840 in the Araguari river region, where nowadays is the state of Amapa. In 1842, the first Infantry Battalion of the Region was created in the city of Belem. Only in 1904 the last conflict in the Brazilian Amazon Region had been solved, with an agreement followed by a treaty that have been signed between Brazil and Bolivia. As a consequence the actual State of Acre was integrated in the Brazilian Territory.

The Army's presence within the Amazon Region reached its highest point in this actual century, with the creation of four Jungle Infantry Brigade, in the states of Para, Rondonia, Roraima and Amazonas, and the Amazon Military Command, in the city of Manaus, capital of the state of Amazonas.

It is important to indicate that this pioneering action has always required unbearable hardships and enormous sacrifices not only from the military institution itself, but also from the

7

individuals and their families who, despite of the hostile environment, have the ideal of protecting the land conquered by their ancestors[15].

Indeed, in some locations, as in most of the border platoons, the military and its family are the only people with roots in developed parts of the country present in the neighborhood, and the only way to reach those areas are by air or by river. Consequently, as the trip by river depends upon the rain season and also may take up to 45 days, most of the support for them is provided by the military, using military aircraft, which are the only ones to fly to those areas.

Thus, the settlement and the development of the Amazon, although still in a slow process, have had as the main actor the Armed Forces, creating in the native population a deep sentiment of the patriotism.

THE INTERNATIONAL COVETOUSNESS

It is fact that some Brazilian development projects of the late sixties, seventies, and part of the eighties in the Amazon Region obeyed a logic which, on the average, proved to be environmentally inadequate or even uneconomic[16]. Taking advantage of this situation, among others, the following attempts to create areas controlled by international organizations can be emphasized:

- The attempt to implement the project "Amazon Great Lakes System", devised in 1967/68 by the Hudson Institute, which would create a multinational lake linking the Amazon and Orinoco river's basin[17]. However, it foresaw the flooding of an area fifteen times larger than all hydroelectric projects planned for the region which were always condemned by ecological groups;

- The "World's Council of Christian Churches", which began its activities in 1981, while addressing the Amazon region and its population, clearly stated in its official guidelines that the Amazon region and its population should not belong to the countries which pretentiously claim them as theirs, but are rather humanity's assets[18];

- The several attempts by the international community for the creation of "Multinational Indians Reservations" in the Amazon region[19].

- The 1989 effort of some "European Politicians" aimed at persuading the European Economic Community to drive the Brazilian Government to interrupt the project "Grande Carajas" (Great Carajas), and thus trying to inhibit the planned search for mineral resources[20];

- The proposal, also in 1989, during the "Haya Conference", by the President of France, to form a supranational environment defense structure which, based on the questionable "premise of shared defense", would have the right to intervene in the Brazilian internal affairs[21]. During the United Nations Conference for Environment (Rio-92), a similar purpose concern to the "limited sovereignty", over the great resources under control of the non-developed countries, has also been addressed[22].

These attempts, along with the fact that the amazon jungle is not the sole large tropical jungle in the world, are eloquent in showing the international greed regarding the amazon region and are concrete evidence worth taking into consideration, especially in issues dealing with the Brazilian sovereignty.

ECOLOGY, MYTHS AND OTHER ISSUES

In the whirlwind of the conservationist movement that has caught the world's attention in the last few years, the extremely sensitive issue of preserving the Amazon region has become emotional.

In order to analyze standpoints, let's do some considerations:

"The Rain Forest"

In Brazil, before the issue of the Amazon comes to the international media, we never heard anything about the "rain forest". Certainly, because that expression doesn't exist in the dictionaries.

Nevertheless, the desinformation campaign related to the interest of some environmental group was so big that it generated a change of the name of the jungle. Suddenly the Amazon Jungle, a tropical forest, was transformed into the "Rain Forest", a real good name to be used to raise money. After all, who wants to save Jungles?[23]

"The World's Lung"

Is it possible to refer to the Amazon region as "the world's lungs"?[24]

When studying the evolution of plants we realize that during the growth period a plant requires less oxygen than it produces, thus, greatly contributing to the environment. However, a forest such as the Amazon has reached its peak developmental stage, also known as the "CLIMAX". In a climax forest, close to the total daily production of oxygen is consumed during the night by its own vegetation, in its respiration process.[25]

There is in fact a very high oxygen production potential in the Amazon region. Ironically, however, in order to allow plants to grow, part of the forest would have to be destroyed. Fortunately, there is no need to report such a measure. The oxygen in the atmosphere became enough for the evolution of air-breathing land animals, some 400 million years ago[26], and for centuries the proportion of the world's oxygen has remained stable (on average 21%)[27], despite much other deforestation that has occurred in the planet.

"Global Warming"

Has the "Global Warming" effect worsened by the wood burning activity in the Amazon region? "Global Warming" is a theory developed by some scientists by which the Earth would be experiencing a warming process due to the excessive emission of carbon dioxide (CO_2) and other kinds of gases produced by combustion[28].

There are, however, scientists with the exact opposite point of view. They argue that the same phenomenon would be responsible for blocking the light and the heat generated by the sun, thus preventing them from reaching the Earth. For them, the planet could be facing a cooling period.

In any instance, the increased release of carbon dioxide (CO_2) into the atmosphere is well documented; wood burning, just like any other form of combustion, do concur to it, as well.

Taken into proportions, however, it needs to be understood that the production of the carbon dioxide by wood burning is minimal. According to scientific studies done so far, the increase of CO_2 is largely because of the practice of burning fossil fuels, coal, and petroleum and its derivatives[29], which occur in bigger proportions in developed nations. We can also emphasize that, during the last 10 years, the world's output of CO_2 exceeded the average of 5 billion tons a year, whereas in brazil all inclusive (forest, fuel, fossil burning, etc.) it reached about 5 million tons a year (approximately 1%).

Desertification

Are large areas of the Amazon region in danger of becoming desert-like because of the deforestation? No scientific evidence backs that hypothesis. In order for the Amazon region to come into a desert-like, a climate change of vast proportions, mainly a change in the wind patterns as to invert the region's precipitation, would have to occur. So far, there is no reliable scientific study indicating such possibility. On the contrary, the observations of the Amazon "jungle" have lead to the conclusion that in all cleared and abandoned areas the forest has showed an incredibly fast renovating power.

Building of Dams

Can large and medium size hydroelectric plants pose serious ecological damage to the Amazon Region? The ecological damage issue needs to be addressed in relation to its proportion to the region's size. All hydroelectric plants planned for the Amazon Region -there are eleven-, which were supposed to be completed by the year 2,010, would flood 0,2% of the area, which relatively speaking it means nothing.

An economy as large as Brazil's cannot be ruled by sentimentalism. People, who argue against the construction of new hydroelectric plants in the Amazon Region, do so as well as when the issue is nuclear plant. Questions on feasible alternatives to a developing country such Brazil, with increasing energy needs, remain unanswered.

Indian rights

Has the Indian population been jeopardized by the development of the Amazon Region? Issues regarding to Brazilian Indians have been discussed even at international levels. As a matter of fact, Brazil has for long years been developing policies oriented towards the preservation and improvement of the lifestyles of its

Indian population. In order to guard the interests of the Indians' population, its preservation, and the protection of its environment against all kinds of aggression, as demanded in the Brazilian Constitution[30], their land demarcation has been accelerated.

In addition to this effort, it is important to emphasize that in Brazil today there are about 330,000 Indians, divided among 220 ethnic groups. This population is settled in more than 500 areas, in a total of 82 million hectares, which is equivalent to 10% of the entire country[31]. This means that each Brazilian Indian is entitled to use close to 400 hectares. In the United States this proportion is set at barely 20 hectares.

Thus, Brazil carries out a serious, responsible, and experienced policy concerning Indian matters. It can be said that among nations, Brazil is the one that invests the most towards Indian preservation and worth. Proving this we can say that the Indians in Brazil are not disappearing; on the contrary, its population is growing at a rate of 3,5 % a year[32].

However, the most interesting fact concerning the Brazilian Indians, is the international pressure to the land demarcation of the "Yanomamis". For a population of about 10,000 Indians, the "ecologists" want Brazilian Government to demarcate an area of about 9 million hectares (bigger than Portugal), or in other words, 900 hectares for each Indian. "Coincidentally", the Yanomami's area is one of the richest in mineral resources of the entire Amazon, having potential, if exploited, to interfere in the balance of the world market of some minerals[33].

Consequently, it is possible to understand why these same governments or NGOs do not show a similar concern about the preservation of the cultures of the tribes in Africa, or the "Miskits" from Nicaragua, or even Brazilian Indians which leave in the South of Brazil... They don't leave on a rich soil[34].

Illegal drug traffic

The commerce of illegal drugs affects all the nations in the world. In this issue, the Amazon attracts attention as potential transit region.

As any other trade, the drugs can be transported in the region through rivers or by air.

Inserted in the international effort against this threat, the Brazilian Federal Police has established "control points" in strategic areas of the rivers in the region, particularly on those which come from the producer countries, allowing more effective surveillance in all traffic made by boat.

Remains the issue of air traffic. The drug cartels often build clandestine airfields to be used by small planes. Although the Brazilian Government has destroyed these airfields, this procedure has not been enough to solve the problem decidedly. To accomplish a permanent solution for the control of the air space in the region, a complex system, called "Protection System for the Amazon", is being developed. The details of this project will be given later. With the control of the rivers and of the air space, the Amazon will no longer be an attractive region for the drugs' transit.

Water pollution

In the Amazon the water pollution is basically related to gold-mining activities, where mercury has been used in gold processing, causing the pollution of some streams. However, there is not gold everywhere in the Amazon. So, the problem is concentrated in sparse areas, without create great consequences. Nevertheless, since 1989 the government has forbidden the use of mercury in this activity and enacted more rigid controls on all commerce of this metal.

Finally, even if we consider the worst hypothesis, the Brazilians would be the ones who suffer, because all the rivers/ streams in the region run into the Brazilian territory.

Management of biodiversity

As a result of misunderstandings when discussing the Amazon, most people around the world consider deforestation as an act of aggression on the jungle. Deforestation figures were also exaggerated as a result of misinterpretation of sensors' information. The analysis of the satellite pictures showed what happened. In fact, burning has occurred mainly in the states of Rondonia, Maranhao, Para and Mato Grosso. Although a portion of the jungle has been destroyed, in these areas we will find mostly natural savannas and a few non-dense forests[35].

16

Data obtained from the "Instituto Nacional de Pesquisas Espaciais" (National Space Research Institute) indicate a decrease in the yearly deforestation rate, from 0.54%/ year during the eighties, to approximately 0.33%/year during this decade (up to 1997). These figures include also the deforestation caused by natural disasters.

The average rate of the jungle clearing rhythm in the Brazilian Amazon Region has decreased since 1983 (the highest deforestation rate ever experienced), a period which include the height of the colonization of the country's northern states.

BRAZILIAN POLICY FOR ENVIRONMENT

Brazil is a State Party to the various international legal agreements adopted in recent years to protect the global environment, including: the Convention on Transboundary Movements of Hazardous Wastes; the Montreal Protocol on the Protection of the Ozone Layer; and the Biodiversity and Climate Change Conventions. Brazil has also a solid legal and institutional framework for the protection of its considerable natural resources and for pollution control and abatement, a process that started in the mid 60's and has continually been updated.

Poverty or economic development cannot be an excuse for environmental aggression. Knowing the area and having a clear understanding of environmental issues have been the Brazilian strategy used to formulate proper policies concerning to the use of the Amazon's resources in the model of the "Sustainable

Development"[36].

The backbone of Brazilian environmental policy is found in the 1988 Constitution and the 1981 National Environment Policy Act. Among its main elements, it stated that[37]:

- the protection of Brazil's environment for present and future generations is a common responsibility of the State and the community;

- every citizen is entitled to a sound environment and to participate in the environmental management process;

- property rights and economic activities must be consistent with, and not detrimental to, the protection of the environment;

- the federal government shall: set standards for environmental quality; issue rules regulating the granting of permits for activities that may pollute or harm the ecosystems where they are carried; and define conservation strategies for the main Brazilian ecosystems (considered "national heritage" under the Constitution). It shall also plan, coordinate and monitor the implementation of the Brazilian Environmental Policy;

- state and local governments have broad regulatory autonomy on matters related to environmental protection and environmental quality initiatives, within the limits set forth by the constitutional provisions and federal legislation in force; most environmental monitoring and licensing activities rest with state and local governments, except when otherwise provided for in the specific legislation.

Biodiversity in the Amazon and the Indian Culture are a natural heritage whose richness Brazil has no intention of either wasting or relinquishing. Reaching a balance between exploring natural resources and preserving the environment for future generations has become the essence of domestic discussions concerning the Amazon.

To implement these policies, which involve ensuring that economic activity in the Amazon is accomplished through the sustainable use of the natural resources of the region, several government Agencies have jurisdiction to develop projects for the area, as we will see in the next sections.

GOVERNMENT ORGANIZATIONS IN THE AREA

Armed Forces

As described before, on the section about the settlement, the most active and ancient governmental institutions in the region have been the Armed Forces. This presence and knowledge of the area have been used to support many other organizations to accomplish their tasks, as we will see ahead.

Ministry of Environment, Water Resources and Legal Amazon

At the federal level, all environment issues concerning to the Amazon Region are under responsibility of the Ministry of Environment, Water Resources and Legal Amazon, which has the following jurisdiction[38]:

-Planning, coordination, supervision, and control of

actions referring to the environment and water resources;

-Formulation and execution of national policy related to the environment and water resources;

-Preservation and conservation, and rational use of renewable natural resources;

-Implementation of international agreements in the environmental area;

-Establishment of an integrated policy for the Legal Amazon.

To carry out its tasks, the Ministry has several bureau and organs. Among them, we can emphasize the following which are important players concerning to the Amazon issues:

a. National Council of the Environment (CONAMA), which has the main following jurisdiction[39]:

- to establish norms and criteria for the licensing of activities effectively or potentially polluting to be granted by the States;

- to determine, when it is considered necessary, the realization of studies of the alternatives and possible environmental consequences of public or private projects;

- to determine, in case of an issue specifically related to the environment, the loss or restriction of fiscal benefits conceded by Public Power, and the loss or suspension of the participation in lines of credit in official credit establishments;

- to establish norms, criteria and patterns pertaining to the control and maintenance of the quality of the environment aiming at the rational use of environmental resources.

b. National Council of the Legal Amazon (CONAMAZ), which has the main following jurisdiction[40]:

- to propose and coordinate the national integrated policy for the Amazon region, together with state and municipal government, taking into account all the dimensions of social and economic life, the basics of the sustainable development, the improvement of the quality of life of the Amazon population, and the protection and preservation of the Amazon environment;

- to follow the implementation of the integrated policy and the coordinated initiatives in the federal area for the Legal Amazon;

- to advise about proposed bills related to the action of the Federal Government in the Legal Amazon;

- to deliberate and propose measures about facts and situations connected to the Legal Amazon, which demand prompt and coordinated action on the part of the Federal Government.

c. National Council of Renewable Natural Resources (CONAREN)[41], which has the main following jurisdiction:

- to formulate the directives of governmental policies regarding the development of the forest, fishing and rubber sectors;

- to propose norms and control patterns for the

exploration, alternative uses, industrialization and commercialization of forest, fishing and rubber products and by-products;

d. National Environment Fund Committee (CFNMA)[42], which has the jurisdiction to develop projects which aim at the rational and sustainable use of natural resources, including the maintenance, improvement, and recovery of environmental quality, so as to raise the quality of life of the Brazilian population.

e. Environmental Issues Coordination Office (SMA), which has the jurisdiction to plan, coordinate, supervise, and control the execution of the national environmental policy.

One of its most important project is the preparation of the "Atlas of the Brazilian Ecosystems and the Main Development Macro-vectors"[43]. It will provide to the sectors that are responsible for the various components of environmental management with a planning tool that will give a more integrated spatial vision, especially with reference to the main development vectors, their characteristics, dynamics and tendencies.

This is the first atlas in the country to collect information about its various economic activities and sectors and their environmental consequences. Information from a great many different sources, such as institutes, ministries and local governments, have been brought together in this document in order to view Brazil's economic development and environmental planning as a whole. The basic idea of the atlas is not to quantify the environmental degradation, but rather to predict, based on the current Brazilian development processes, and to anticipate the environmental degradation and impact processes.

For this purpose, the research has been focused on the following macro-vectors: agribusiness, energy utilization, industrialization, urbanization, circulation, fishing exploitation, forest exploitation, mineral exploitation, and international flows. These nine selected themes represent basically those activities that have greater direct repercussions on land occupation, on the exploitation of renewable and non-renewable natural resources and the various dynamics of environmental change in general.

f. Legal Amazon Issues Coordination Office (SCA)[44], which has the jurisdiction to coordinate, supervise and follow the actions related to the national integrated policy for the Legal Amazon, and to give the necessary technical and administrative support to the functioning of the National Council of the Legal Amazon.

g. Water Resources Office (SRH)[45], which has the jurisdiction to plan, supervise, control, execute and make execute the National Water Resources Policy and the policy of Hydroagricultural use, and orient, promote and cooperate with public and private entities in the realization of research and studies destined to the sustainable use of water resources.

h. Institute of the Environment and Renewable Natural Resources (IBAMA)[46]. It is a special federal agency, with a public law juridical personality, possessing administrative and financial autonomy, which has as its aim to formulate, coordinate, execute and see to the execution the national environmental policy and the preservation, conservation, and rational use, inspection, control and promoting of renewable natural resources.

It is the main instrument that allow the Ministry to exercise two of the major challenges of the environmental policy:

- education, which has the objective to create in each person the mentality of development without degradation; and

- inspection, that requires a large amount of resources, equipment and personnel, to operate in an ample and harmful area.

Ministry of Justice

Concerning to the Amazon issues, this Ministry has jurisdiction related to the protection of the Indians, security of the borders and counter-drug operations. To execute its tasks it has the following Bureaus:

a. Indian National Foundation (FUNAI)[47]. It is an organ which establish and execute the Brazilian Indian policy, according to what is stated in the National Constitution. Besides the headquarters, the Foundation has 47 regional administrations, which have to implement the following tasks:

- to exert, on behalf of the Government, the custody of

24

the Indians and its communities;

      - to guarantee the fulfillment of the Indians' policy, including the preservation of the biological and cultural equilibrium and the identity of the Indians on their liaison with the national society;

      - to manage the indigenous patrimony, aiming it conservation, enlargement and valorization;

      - to promote surveys, analysis, studies and scientific research about the Indians, aiming the preservation of the culture and the appropriateness of the assistance programs;

      - to promote medical-sanitary assistance to the Indians;

      - to promote the appropriate base education to the Indians;

      - to promote the development of their community;

Nevertheless, because of the changes in the Indian's policy established in the Constitution of 1988, and the deficiency of resources, the FUNAI hasn't been able to accomplish its entire mission. To assist in this issue, an agreement has been established between Brazilian Government and the "Group of Seven", that has allowed the G7 to contribute with some monetary support since 1991.

b. Federal Police Bureau

With an area of action that comprise all country, the Federal Police Department[48], which is attached at the structure of the

Ministry of the Justice, has its jurisdiction established at the federal Constitution of 1988. As the main responsibility, related to the Amazon Region, we can emphasize:

- to prevent or repress the illicit traffic of drugs, the contraband...;

- to exercise the function of maritime, aerial and border police;

To facilitate the fulfillment of their tasks, some complementary legislation have given to them also the right to investigate the "organized crime" and to control all commerce of chemical products which can be used on the drug's processing.

To accomplish its main task in the region - elimination of illegal drug traffic - the Federal Police, with support of another governmental agencies, mainly the Armed Forces, established strategic bases that have allowed the control of the navigation on the major rivers. Concerning to the illegal traffic of small planes, the clandestine airfields have been put out of action as soon as they are identified. However, the total control of the air traffic will only be secured after the implementation of the SIVAM project, which we will explain ahead.

GOVERNMENT PROJECTS IN THE AREA

Project "Calha Norte" (North Channel)

Project "Calha Norte"[49] is a federal government initiative aimed at effectively integrating the northern region of the channels of the Solimões and Amazonas Rivers into the National

26

Context.

The program was launched in 1985 once the importance of the area, particularly at the international level, was perceived. In 1986, the program was already operative. It anticipated a joint and coordinated endeavor by various ministries and government agencies towards the following goals:

- to improve the Brazilian presence in the area, thus intensifying government related job opportunities, in order to encourage the region's development;

- to increase bilateral relations with neighboring countries, strengthen cooperation mechanisms and production determinants, reinforce consular offices and facilitate trade among borderland population;

- to expand the roadways infra-structure without interfering in the region's natural trend, i.e., its fluvial transportation, the most important means of regional integration;

- to empower government agencies, such as the justice department, federal police, internal revenue, and social security offices, to act as inhibitors of unlawful practices springing from the small presence of the government in distant and isolated areas;

- to intensify boundary demarcation campaigns thereby restoring and consolidating bordering landmarks;

- to promote the assistance and protection of Indian, riverside, and extractor populations through the delimitation and demarcation of Indian lands and through the establishment of national forests capable of offering them natural protection in light of cultural contrasts.

To carry out the project, the first step was to ensure the occupation of the area, basically through the Armed Forces. Brigades were moved from the south of Brazil and became "Jungle Infantry Brigades". In addition, some Platoons have been established (18 so far) in strategic areas along the border.

Simultaneously, other government agencies have been responsible for improving the infrastructure in the region, in form to create better life conditions, which would contribute to attract the people to come and stay there. These infrastructure initiatives include health care, schools, water and sanitary systems, communication system, etc.

Nevertheless, as we said before, in those isolated platoons the main population is still the military and its families.

Amazon Protect System (SIPAM)

Based on the awareness that the resources available were insufficient for the Brazilians to collect data and generate useful knowledge on the region's potentialities, limitations, and realities, the Brazilian Government decided to create the Amazon Protect System (SIPAM)[50]. The SIPAM is an integrated system that involves several government organizations, from which the flow of information will allow the government to have a global vision of the problems in the Amazon and, as a consequence, to provide a

28

more appropriate response according to the real necessities of the region. The main technical support of the SIPAM is the "System for Vigilance of the Amazon" (SIVAM)[51].

The SIVAM is an operational system that will employ means – equipment, software and personnel – with the objective to collect, process, produce, and diffuse data about the Amazon which are of interest of the components of the SIPAM. The SIVAM program was conceived in 1990 and announced to world leaders at the Rio' 92 Conference. With a total cost equivalent to about 1.4 billion US dollars, it will be composed of a large quantity of sensors – from stationary radars to satellites – and remote user stations connected to regional coordination centers by a vast and encompassing telecommunications network, to gather extensive data from the Amazon region. These data will include the wide range of problems in the area, such as: illegal gold mining, deforestation, drug production and traffic, smuggling, and conflicts over land use between the indigenous people of the Amazon and more recent settlers.

SIVAM's objective[52] is therefore the implementation of a surveillance and analysis infrastructure that will provide the Brazilian Government with the necessary information for the protection and sustainable development of the Amazon region. The information generated by SIVAM is going to aid governmental organizations and other users in the execution of tasks such as:

-environmental protection

-control of land occupation and usage

-economical and ecological zoning

-updating of maps

-prevention and control of epidemics

-protection of the indigenous populations

-surveillance and control of the borders

-monitoring of river navigation and forest fires

-identification and combat against illegal activities

-air traffic surveillance and control.

In March of 1997 the five contracts for external financing were signed and in July the activities for implementation had started.

SIVAM will be completely implemented within five years. However, by the end of the third year, a large part of the sensors and the Regional Center in Manaus will already be available. Besides this, during the first year, a Prototype Development Center will offer to future users conditions to develop applications and programs through sensor simulations.

At the end of 1997, from the total 25 radars of the entire system, 9 have been already working. To have an idea of the number of the small airplanes that fly in the Amazon, one of the newly installed radars, in its first month of experimental activity, detected more than 300 air traffic unknown from the air traffic control[53].

Although the main hardware have been imported, SIVAM is being installed with important participation of the Brazilian industry and technicians and will be operated exclusively by Brazilians with use of Brazilian software, thus conserving the strategic destination of Brazilian resources in Brazilian hands. According to Col. Antonio Faria, commission chief of the SIVAM Project, "when the system be completely installed, the Amazon will be better supervised than all other part in Brazil"[54].

Other resolutions

In addition to the presence in the area, and these main programs that have been developed, the Brazilian government has deliberated about many subjects which, as a whole, represent important steps to the idea of a sustainable development for that region. Among others, we can emphasize the following:

a. Establishment of the Amazon Agroforestry Research Center (CPAA)[55]. Its mandate is to develop and diffuse technologies for the sustainable development of the region through the rational utilization and conservation of renewable natural resources. In addition to its own projects, the CPAA develops joint research proposals with a variety of foreign universities and international agencies such as:

- University of Hamburg - GERMAN;

- University of Florida - USA;

- North Carolina State University - USA;

- Center for Tropical Agriculture (CIAT);

- Center for International Agriculture Research.

31

b. To intensify the monitoring of activities by annually surveying the entire Amazon region[56].

c. Alteration of the Forestry Code that enlarged from 50% to 80% the area secured under the law on rural properties in the "Legal Amazon" region with vegetative ground cover. As a result, on properties that contain forests, deforestation of more than 20% of their area is not permitted[57].

d. Properties that already contain deforested areas that are abandoned, under-used or used inappropriately cannot be authorized for additional clearing of their lands[58].

e. It has been an obligation, in those areas with indigenous vegetative ground cover, to implement sustainable management for multiple use[59].

f. Implantation of a system (SIAMAZ)[60] which integrates the Amazonian Universities. It is a computerized network of information system in the framework of the Amazonian countries-Bolivia, Brazil, Colombia, Ecuador, Guyana, Peru, Surinam and Venezuela.

The System is structured to integrate information units and to share resources (under the coordination of each national network), operating according to a common set of norms, mechanisms and methodologies, circulating the information generated in and about the region.

g. Encourage the continuation of multinational projects through the Amazon National Research Institute (INPA), which will allow a better understanding of the Amazon environment[61].

h. Increase the interagency operations in the Amazon to prevent illegal deforestation, drug traffic, etc.

i. The approval by the Congress, in January of 1998, of a new law that increase the fine and establishes other punishments tools for crimes against the environment[62].

CONCLUSION

Brazilians inherited the immense Amazon region, accounting for over half of the entire country, which, by its special characteristics, distance, and isolation from more populated areas, has for a long time remained fairly unknown and thinly explored. The region is, nevertheless, a Brazilian asset that definitively needs to be understood as such. Our people have dwelled in that region for over 350 years since its discovery, and much sacrifice and bloodshed went into keeping it that way. Pressing challenges lie ahead in the process of humanizing and developing the Amazon region, particularly when it comes to the defense of natural ecological systems and to the incorporation of adequate agricultural techniques to humid tropics.

These challenges cannot, however, serve as obstacles to the rational utilization of the region. To keep the Amazon region untouched, as nature's sanctuary, is an absurdity only imaginable to dreamers or to those without responsibility towards the future of our country or the interests of our people. To ignore the existence of such a vast unexplored region at the expense of a large segment of Brazilians, who live miserably, unable to fulfill the least necessary requirements to carry on a dignified life, seems to us as being somewhat out of focus.

The preservation of nature is an important subject. Even so, we do believe it is feasible to shun two extremes: an untouched territory or total devastation.

We can also adduce that many who engage in talks about the Amazon region have never even visited the region. In consequence, it is of utmost importance that this extensive region of our country be better known, since only then will many false concepts be settled and the region's problems, better understood, more adequately addressed and resolved, thus providing the necessary defenses against international greed.

> "It would be unrealistic to suppose that certain resources pertain to humanity as a whole, while in fact they are located within national borders. If it were accepted that they be shared in a kind of "world fund", it would be no less correct to expect that economic, political and technological authority also be shared by all nations. Since the central countries do not appear to be willing to accept this later idea, the peripheral countries are to an even lesser degree willing to renounce their right to decide how to use their natural resources"[63].

Many are the challenges to be overcome in pursuit of this aspiration, particularly in the matter of natural ecological systems' defense, ensuring that human activities do not overload the carrying capacity of each ecosystem. Those are challenges to the creativity, the perseverance and the patriotism of the Brazilian people.   (Total words = 7053)

ENDNOTES

[1] Antonio A. Dayrell de Lima, "Environment and Globalization: a Brazilian view," December 95; available from <http://www. brasil.emb.nw.dc.us/evar02li.htm>; Internet; accessed 16 Oct 97.

[2] The ideas in this paragraph are based in a lecture prepared by Comando Militar da Amazonia (Brazilian Regional Commander of Amazon), about "O Exercito na Amazonia" ("The Army in the Amazon). Manaus, AM, 1996.

[3] Instituto Nacional de Pesquisas Espaciais, "Monitorando a floresta," January 98; available from <http://www.inpe.br/amz-01-11.htm>; Internet; accessed 12 Feb 98.

[4] Editora Abril, Almanaque Abril 97. Sao Paulo, SP, 96 and 643.

[5] Fundacao Nacional do Indio; available from <http://www. funai.gov.br>; Internet; accessed 23 Dec 97.

[6] Editora Abril, Almanaque Abril 97, 205.

[7] Comando Militar da Amazonia, lecture.

[8] Comando Militar da Amazonia, lecture.

[9] Instituto Nacional de Pesquisas Espaciais.

[10] Editora Abril, Almanaque Abril 97, 98.

[11] Gelio Fregapani, Amazonia 1996 - Soberania Ameacada (Amazon 1996 - Sovereignty Threatened) (Brasilia, DF: Thesaurus, 1995), 22-26.

[12] Alvaro de Souza Pinheiro and William W. Mendel, Guerrilla in the Brazilian Amazon (Kansas, Fort Leavenworth, 1995), 01.

[13] Ibid.

[14] According to the "Tordesillas Treaty", signed between Portugal and Spain in the XV century, the Amazon Region was in the west of the Meridian (Spanish side).

[15] Comando Militar da Amazonia, lecture.

[16] Lima.

[17] Correio Braziliense (Brazilian Newspaper), 21 April 1989, p.4.

[18] Osmar Jose de Barros Ribeiro, "Amazonia - Um Desafio a Vencer," A Defesa Nacional, no 768 (April/May/June 1995): 57.

[19] Fregapani, 51-58.

[20] Andrew Hurrel, "Brazil and the International Politics of Amazonian Deforestation," in The International Politics of the Environment, ed. Andrew Hurrel and Benedict Kingsbury (Oxford: Clarendon Press, 1992), 417.

[21] Ibid, 406.

[22] Comando Militar da Amazonia, lecture.

[23] Luis Carlos Guedes, Brazil, the Present Situation and the Effects in the Armed Forces (Washington, D.C., National Defense University, 1993), 07.

[24] Lima.

[25] Microsoft Encarta 97 Encyclopedia, (Microsoft Corporation, CD-ROM, 1997), Process of Respiration.

[26] Ibid, Atmosphere.

[27] Ibid, Oxygen.

[28] Ibid, Environment.

[29] Ibid.

[30] Brazilian Congress, Constitution of the Republic of Brazil, (Brasilia, October 1988), art. 231.

[31] Fundacao Nacional do Indio.

[32] Bruno Paes Manso, "Eles Resistem," Veja (Amazonia, Special Edition), 24 Dec 97.

[33] The ideas in this paragraph are based on remarks made by a speaker participating in a Symposium about the Brazilian Amazon. ECEME, Rio de Janeiro, RJ, October 1991.

[34] Fregapani, 51-58.

[35] Pedro Aramis de Lima Arruda, Brazilian Rain Forest. Security. Environment. Development (Carlisle Barracks, PA, U.S. Army War College, 10 Mar 1993), 23.

[36] Ibid, 27.

[37] Brazilian Embassy, "Environmental Law and Environmental Business Oportunities in Brazil: An Overview," 1994; available from <http://www.brasil.emb.nw.dc.us/amb-biz.htm>; Internet; accessed 16 Oct 97.

[38] Brazilian Ministry of Environment, Water Resources and Legal Amazon, "Jurisdiction of the Ministry;" available from <http://www.mma.gov.br/ingles/CGMI/compti.html>; Internet; accessed 23 Dec 97.

[39] Ibid, "CONAMA;" available from <http://www.mma.gov.br/ingles/CGMI/consi.html>; Internet; accessed 23 Dec 97.

[40] Ibid, "CONAMAZ;" available from <http://www.mma.gov.br/ingles/CGMI/consli.html>; Internet; accessed 23 Dec 97.

[41] Ibid, "CONAREN;" available from <http://www.mma.gov.br/ingles/CGMI/cons2i.html>; Internet; accessed 23 Dec 97.

[42] Ibid, "CFNMA;" available from <http://www.mma.gov.br/ingles/CGMI/comi.html>; Internet; accessed 23 Dec 97.

[43] Ibid, "Atlas of the Brazilian Ecosystems and the Main Development Macro-Vectors;" available from <http://www.mma.gov.br/ingles/SMA/atlas/atlasi.html>; Internet; accessed 23 Dec 97.

[44] Ibid, "SCA;" available from <http://www.mma.gov.br/ingles/CGMI/sec1ai.html>; Internet; accessed 23 Dec 97.

[45] Ibid, "SRH;" available from <http://www.mma.gov.br/ingles/CGMI/sec3i.html>; Internet; accessed 23 Dec 97.

[46] Ibid, "IBAMA;" available from <http://www.mma.gov.br/ingles/CGMI/ibamai.html>; Internet; accessed 23 Dec 97.

[47] Fundacao Nacional do Indio.

[48] Brazilian Federal Police Department, "Coodenacao Central de Policia;" available from <http://www.dpf.gov.br/ccp.htm>; Internet; accessed 23 Dec 97.

[49] Brazilian Secretariat of Strategic Affairs, "Programa Calha Norte;" available from <http://www.sae.gov.br/spp/pcn1.htm>; Internet; accessed 16 Oct 97.

[50] Ibid, "SIPAM;" available from <http://www.sae.gov.br/cisipam/sipam.htm>; Internet; accessed 16 Oct 97.

[51] Ibid, "SIVAM;" available from <http://www.sae.gov.br/cisipam/sivam.htm>; Internet; accessed 16 Oct 97.

[52] Raytheon Eletronic Systems, "System for Vigilance of the Amazon," 1996; available from <http://www.raytheon.com/sivam/sivameng.html>; Internet; accessed 16 Oct 97.

[53] Brazilian Secretariat of Strategic Affairs, "SIPAM/SIVAM, A Situacao Atual;" available from <http://www.sae.gov.br/cisipam/atual.htm>; Internet; accessed 16 Oct 97.

[54] Leonel Rocha, "O Espiao da Floresta," Veja (Amazonia, Special Edition), 24 Dec 97.

[55] Brazilian Agricultural Research Corporation, "CPAA," 1996; available from <http://www.cr-am.rnp.br/embrapa/fcpaa.html>; Internet; accessed 16 Oct 97.

[56] Brazilian Embassy, "Information on Amazon Deforestation," 1991-1994; available from <http://www.brasil.emb.nw.dc.us/evar03df.htm>; Internet; accessed 16 Oct 97.

[57] Ibid.

[58] Ibid.

[59] Ibid.

[60] Fernando Elarrat and Ivan Listo, "SIAMAZ," 1996; available from <http://www.interconect.com.br/siamaz/oqueei.htm>; Internet; accessed 16 Oct 97.

[61] Instituto Nacional de Pesquisas da Amazonia, "INPA;" available from <http://www.cr-am.rnp.br/inpahome.html>; Internet; accessed 16 Oct 97.

[62] Folha de Sao Paulo (Brazilian Newspaper), 29 Jan 98.

[63] Interministerial Commission for the Preparation of the United Nations Conference on Environment and Development, The Challenge of Sustainable Development, (Brasilia, DF: Secretariat of the Presidency of the Republic of Brazil Press, 1992), 20.

BIBLIOGRAPHY

Arruda, Pedro Aramis de Lima. Brazilian Rain Forest. Security. Environment. Development. Carlisle Barracks, PA, U.S. Army War College, 10 Mar 1993.

Brazilian Agricultural Research Corporation. "CPAA," 1996. Available from <http://www.cr-am.rnp.br/embrapa/fcpaa.html>. Internet. Accessed 16 Oct 97

Brazilian Congress, Constitution of the Republic of Brazil. Brasilia, October 1988.

Brazilian Embassy. "Environmental Law and Environmental Business Opportunities in Brazil: An Overview," 1994. Available from <http://www. brasil.emb.nw.dc.us/amb-biz.htm>. Internet. Accessed 16 Oct 97.

_____. "Information on Amazon Deforestation," 1991-1994. Available from <http://www.brasil.emb.nw.dc.us/evar03df.htm>. Internet. Accessed 16 Oct 97.

Brazilian Federal Police Department. "Coordenacao Central de Policia." Available from <http://www.dpf.gov.br/ccp.htm>. Internet. Accessed 23 Dec 97.

Brazilian Ministry of Environment, Water Resources and Legal Amazon. "Atlas of the Brazilian Ecosystems and the Main Development Macro-Vectors." Available from <http://www.mma. gov.br/ingles/SMA/atlas/atlasi.html>. Internet. Accessed 23 Dec 97.

_____."CFNMA." Available from <http://www.mma.gov.br/ingles/ CGMI/comi.html>. Internet. Accessed 23 Dec 97.

_____."CONAMA." Available from <http://www.mma.gov.br/ ingles/CGMI/consi.html>. Internet. Accessed 23 Dec 97.

_____."CONAMAZ." Available from <http://www.mma.gov.br/ ingles/CGMI/consli.html>. Internet. Accessed 23 Dec 97.

_____."CONAREN." Available from <http://www.mma.gov.br/ ingles/CGMI/cons2i.html>. Internet. Accessed 23 Dec 97.

_____."IBAMA." Available from <http://www.mma.gov.br/ingles/ CGMI/ibamai.html>. Internet. Accessed 23 Dec 97.

_____."Jurisdiction of the Ministry." Available from <http:// www.mma.gov.br/ingles/CGMI/compti.html>. Internet. Accessed 23 Dec 97.

_____."SCA." Available from <http://www.mma.gov.br/ingles/ CGMI/sec1ai.html>. Internet. Accessed 23 Dec 97.

_____."SRH." Available from <http://www.mma.gov.br/ingles/ CGMI/sec3i.html>. Internet. Accessed 23 Dec 97.

Brazilian Secretariat of Strategic Affairs. "Programa Calha Norte." Available from <http://www.sae.gov.br/spp/pcn1.htm>. Internet. Accessed 16 Oct 97.

_____."SIPAM." Available from <http://www.sae.gov.br/cisipam/ sipam.htm>. Internet. Accessed 16 Oct 97.

_____."SIPAM/SIVAM, A Situacao Atual." Available from <http:// www.sae.gov.br/cisipam/atual.htm>. Internet. Accessed 16 Oct 97.

_____."SIVAM." Available from <http://www.sae.gov.br/cisipam/ sivam.htm>. Internet. Accessed 16 Oct 97.

Correio Braziliense (Brazilian Newspaper), 21 April 1989, p.4.

Editora Abril. Almanaque Abril 97. Sao Paulo, SP, 1997.

Elarrat, Fernando and Ivan Listo. "SIAMAZ," 1996. Available from <http://www.interconect.com.br/siamaz/oqueei.htm>. Internet. Accessed 16 Oct 97.

Encyclopedia, Microsoft Encarta 97. Microsoft Corporation, CD-ROM, 1997.

Folha de Sao Paulo (Brazilian Newspaper). 29 Jan 98.

Fregapani, Gelio. Amazonia 1996 - Soberania Ameacada (Amazon 1996 - Sovereignty Threatened). Brasilia, DF: Thesaurus, 1995.

Fundacao Nacional do Indio. Available from <http://www. funai.gov.br>. Internet. Accessed 23 Dec 97.

Goldblatt, David. Social theory and the environment. Boulder: Westview Press, 1996.

Guedes, Luis Carlos. Brazil, the Present Situation and the Effects in the Armed Forces. Washington, D.C., National Defense University, 1993.

Hurrel, Andrew. "Brazil and the International Politics of Amazonian Deforestation." In The International Politics of the Environment, ed. Andrew Hurrel and Benedict Kingsbury, 398-429. Oxford: Clarendon Press, 1992.

Instituto Nacional de Pesquisas da Amazonia. "INPA." Available from <http://www.cr-am.rnp.br/inpahome.html>. Internet. Accessed 16 Oct 97.

Instituto Nacional de Pesquisas Espaciais, "Monitorando a floresta," January 98. Available from <http://www.inpe.br/amz-01-11.htm>. Internet. Accessed 12 Feb 98.

Interministerial Commission for the Preparation of the United Nations Conference on Environment and Development. The Challenge of Sustainable Development. Brasilia, DF: Secretariat of the Presidency of the Republic of Brazil Press, 1992.

Lima, Antonio A. Dayrell de. "Environment and Globalization: a Brazilian view," December 95. Available from <http://www.brasil.emb.nw.dc.us/evar021i.htm>. Internet. Accessed 16 Oct 97.

Manso, Bruno Paes. "Eles Resistem." Veja (Amazonia, Special Edition), 24 Dec 97.

Pinheiro, Alvaro de Souza, and William W. Mendel. Guerrilla in the Brazilian Amazon. Kansas, Fort Leavenworth, 1995.

Raytheon Electronic Systems. "System for Vigilance of the Amazon," 1996 Available from <http://www.raytheon.com/sivam/sivameng.html>. Internet. Accessed 16 Oct 97.

Ribeiro, Osmar Jose de Barros. "Amazonia - Um Desafio a Vencer." A Defesa Nacional, no 768 (April/May/June 1995): 49-61.

Rocha, Leonel. "O Espiao da Floresta." Veja (Amazonia, Special Edition), 24 Dec 97.

www.ingramcontent.com/pod-product-compliance
Lightning Source LLC
Chambersburg PA
CBHW081127280526
45787CB00007B/3006